NEBRASKA

in words and pictures

BY DENNIS B. FRADIN

ILLUSTRATIONS BY RICHARD WAHL

MAPS BY LEN W. MEENTS

Consultant
    Paul C. Andreas
    Nebraska History
    Westside High School
    Omaha, Nebraska

 CHILDRENS PRESS ®

CHICAGO

To Anthony Fradin, tough as a pioneer

Nebraska National Forest

Library of Congress Cataloging in Publication Data

Fradin, Dennis B.
  Nebraska in words and pictures.

  SUMMARY: A brief introduction to the history,
people, places of interest, and major cities of the
"Cornhusker State."
  1. Nebraska—Juvenile literature. [1. Nebraska]
I. Wahl, Richard, 1939-   II. Meents, Len W.
III. Title.
F666.3.F7   978.2'03   79-19456
ISBN 0-516-03927-X

Picture Acknowledgments:
NEBRASKA DEPARTMENT OF ECONOMIC DEVELOPMENT: cover, 2,
10, 13, 15, 19 (right), 20, 23, 24, 25, 27, 28, 29, 30, 31, 33, 34, 35, 36, 38,
39, 40, 42
THE HASTINGS AREA CHAMBER OF COMMERCE, INC.: 17, 19 (left)
LINCOLN CHAMBER OF COMMERCE: 32

COVER PICTURE: Nebraska farmland

Nebraska

Nebraska (neh • BRASS • kuh) comes from the Oto

(OD • o •) Indian word *Nebrathka.* It means *flat water.*

That was the name the Otos had for the Platte (PLAT)

River, which is Nebraska's main river.

Nebraska is near the middle of the United States. It is

a big state—the fifteenth biggest. Compared to most

states, Nebraska has few people—just one and one-half

million.

Nebraska has a lot of flat grassland. Nebraska has

many farms where corn and wheat are grown. It has

ranches where cattle are raised.

Do you know where President Gerald Ford was born? Do you know where a famous home for boys—Boys Town—is located? Do you know where the world's largest mammoth skeleton was found?

As you will learn, the answer to all these questions is—Nebraska.

Before people lived in Nebraska there were interesting animals. Mammoths lived in Nebraska. They looked like big, hairy elephants. Mammoths had long, curved tusks. One huge mammoth skeleton was found near North Platte. It is over 13 feet tall. It is the largest mammoth skeleton ever found.

Giant beavers also lived in Nebraska. They were as big as a grown man. Bones of giant beavers have been found in Nebraska to prove this.

Mammoths and giant beavers died out long ago.

The first people came to live in Nebraska at least 12,000 years ago. One early group is called the Folsom Culture (FOL • sum KUL • cher). They lived in western Nebraska. They made spears. They made bows and arrows. They hunted giant bison and mammoths.

In eastern Nebraska the early people learned to farm. Their farm tools and needles were made of bone. They made pottery, too.

In more recent times at least eight Indian tribes lived in Nebraska. Indians in the east were mainly farmers. Those in the west were mainly hunters.

The Pawnee (paw • NEE) were the largest tribe. They lived in southern and eastern Nebraska. They were

mainly farmers. They planted corn, beans, and melons in
the spring. Then all summer they went off to hunt
buffalo. The summer rains helped the crops grow. When
the Pawnee returned from their hunt in September, the
crops were ready to be harvested.

The Pawnee Indians lived in villages. Each village was
run by chiefs. Pawnee houses—called *lodges*—were made
of mud, wood, and grass. When the Pawnee went out to
hunt they took tepees with them. Tepees were tents
made out of animal skins.

Other tribes in eastern Nebraska were the Ponca (PON • ka), Oto, Omaha (oh • MA • haw), and Missouri (meh • ZUR • ree). They were peaceful people who grew crops.

The Sioux (SUE) Indians were hunters who lived in the west and north. They traveled across the land hunting buffalo. They did not farm. They were more fierce than the farming Indians—especially if they found others on their hunting grounds. The Sioux and the Pawnee often fought each other. Three of the great Sioux chiefs were Red Cloud, Spotted Tail, and Crazy Horse.

Besides the Sioux Indians, other tribes that roamed through western Nebraska were the Cheyenne (SHY • ann), Comanche (ka • MAN • chee), and Arapaho (ah • RAP • a • ho). At one time about 40,000 Indians lived in Nebraska.

The Spanish were the first outsiders in Nebraska. In 1541 the Spanish explorer Coronado traveled through the region. He was looking for a city made of gold. It was called *Quivera* (que • VAIR • ha). Coronado and his soldiers did not find it. Coronado did meet with some Indians, however.

The stories of the city of gold did not die. Other Spanish explorers came to Nebraska, looking for gold. Based on these explorations, Spain claimed Nebraska.

Although the king of Spain claimed Nebraska, few Spanish people came there. They saw that there was no city of gold. So they had little interest.

The French were more interested. In 1682 the French explorer La Salle claimed a huge area of America for France. This area included Nebraska. French fur traders came to Nebraska. These men traded pots, beads, guns, and trinkets to the Indians. In return they received

animal furs. Deer, mink, antelope, and beaver were some
of the fur-bearing animals in Nebraska. Fur traders sold
the furs for a lot of money. The furs were made into
fancy clothes.

The French made friends with some Pawnee Indians.
The Spanish and the French began to fight over the land.
In one battle, the Pawnee Indians attacked the Spanish
and defeated them. The Spanish leader Pedro de Villasur
(vee • YAH • sewer) was killed in this battle. For much of
the 1700s, France claimed Nebraska.

The Platte River

French explorers came to Nebraska. In 1714 the French explorer de Bourgmont (BORG • mont) explored the mouth of the Platte River. In 1739 two French brothers—Paul and Pierre Mallet (PEE • air mal • LAY)—traveled across Nebraska. They gave the Platte River its name. It means *shallow water* in French.

At times the water in the middle of the Platte River is very shallow. It is no deeper than the water in your bathtub!

The land called *Nebraska* passed back and forth between Spain and France. In 1762 Spain gained control. But then in 1800 France regained control. Except for Indians, there were still mostly fur traders in Nebraska in 1800. No gold was found in Nebraska. People didn't yet realize that Nebraska had something worth more than any gold mine: lots of great farm land.

In 1776 a new country had been formed in America—the United States of America. In 1803 the United States bought a big piece of land—including Nebraska—from France. The United States wanted to learn more about this land it had bought. In 1804 President Thomas Jefferson sent two explorers out to this new land.

The explorers were Meriwether (MER • ee • WEH • ther) Lewis and William (Will • yum) Clark. They explored many places, including parts of Nebraska. They went up the Missouri River. They explored rivers in eastern Nebraska. They met with friendly Oto and Missouri Indians.

Word spread that Nebraska was a good place for fur traders to deal with the Indians. Manuel Lisa (mon • WELL LEE • sah) built trading posts in Nebraska. One post, Fort Lisa, was ten miles from where Omaha is today. It was founded in 1812. Later, the American Fur Company built trading posts in Nebraska. Forts, such as Fort Atkinson, were built to protect American fur traders. Later, forts like Fort Kearny (CAR • nee) were built to protect settlers traveling across America.

In the 1840s thousands of people in covered wagons traveled through Nebraska. A famous trail, the Oregon (or • eh • GUN) Trail, went through Nebraska. It was just south of the Platte River. The Mormon Trail was just north of the Platte River. Families in covered wagons traveled on these dirt trails. Many wagons made up a "wagon train." Some of the wagons were pulled by oxen. The pioneers carried everything they owned in their wagon. The people shot buffalo and antelope for food.

They were traveling through unknown land. They had to cross rivers. They had to find drinking water. They were lucky if they made 20 miles in a day. Many died of disease on the trip. Chimney Rock, in western Nebraska, was like a signpost to the pioneers. Once here, they knew they had to travel into mountainous country.

The pioneers weren't allowed to set up farms in Nebraska. Nebraska was Indian land. The pioneers were

Chimney Rock

supposed to be traveling *through* Nebraska. Some of the pioneers were going to California (kal • ah • FORN • yah) to look for gold. Others were going to farm in Oregon or Washington. But some liked the look of Nebraska. They settled there—even though it was against the law.

Now the word spread: "There's great farm land in Nebraska!" In 1854 Nebraska was made into a territory. Now people were allowed to set up farms in Nebraska. People began coming *to* Nebraska. Also, many people hadn't found gold in California. They remembered the good farm land they had seen in Nebraska. They returned there to set up farms. In 1854, 2,732 settlers lived in Nebraska. By 1860, 28,841 settlers lived there.

The pioneers who made it to Nebraska were tough. They were strong. It had been a rough trip by covered wagon to get to Nebraska. Things were no easier once they arrived. There were few trees on the Nebraska plains. So the pioneers couldn't build log cabins.

North, south, east, and west—everywhere the pioneers looked they saw nothing but the hard ground, covered by tall grass. There seemed to be no way to build a house. But they figured out a way. They used the tough ground—called *sod*—to build their houses. How? They cut the grassy sod into blocks. Then they piled the sod blocks up, like bricks. With a lot of hard work a pioneer family could make a nice-looking house. They called these houses "soddies." The roof of a soddy was often made of weeds and sod. The pioneers used animal skins to cover the windows. The floor was often just the dirt. In the spring, wild flowers often grew on the roofs of the houses.

Sod house

Pioneers usually settled near rivers. That way they and their livestock would have water. Where many pioneers settled in one place, towns grew. Bellevue, Nebraska City, and Omaha City (later Omaha) were three of those growing towns.

The Nebraska settlers grew corn. It was hard to plant. That brick-hard ground—good for making soddies—was tough to plow. Farmers broke up the ground as best they could with wooden plows. Sometimes they just took hoes to break up the ground. Then they dropped the seeds into the ground by hand. Pioneers also grew wheat, oats, potatoes, and melons.

The government tried to get people to go westward to places like Nebraska. In 1862 the Homestead Act was passed by the U.S. Congress. People could now get 160 acres of free land in Nebraska. In return, the people had to live on the land for five years and work it. One of the first homesteaders was Daniel Freeman. He built a farm near Beatrice (bee • AH • triss). Because of the free land, people poured in. Between 1860 and 1870 almost 100,000 people came. In 1867, on March 1, Nebraska became the 37th state. The capital was Lincoln.

Nebraska had a lot of corn. The corn had to have the husks taken off. Many small towns had cornhusking contests, to make the work fun. So Nebraska earned the nickname the *Cornhusker State.*

Rows of soybeans

Nebraskans worked hard to improve their new state. They wanted their children to have wooden houses, not sod ones. So they planted trees. Soon Nebraska earned another nickname: the *Tree Planters' State.*

Towns were quickly built. The Nebraska pioneers gave their towns interesting names. Broken Bow got its name when a homesteader found a broken bow at an Indian burial ground. Beatrice was named after a young girl whose father helped found the town.

People in Nebraska and the rest of the West were finding it hard to travel over the old trails. Train tracks were laid. By 1867 the Union Pacific Railroad crossed Nebraska. Other railroads were built. Now people—and cattle—could travel by train. Nebraskans built better roads in their state. The telegraph, then the telephone, came to Nebraska. Now people could talk over long distances.

The Union Pacific Railroad

The Indians hadn't minded when people had come to trade with them. Now they saw that the Americans wanted to take the land—all the land. The Indians grew angry.

The railroad builders killed buffalo for food. So there were less buffalo to hunt. The farmers were fencing off the Indians' hunting grounds. The U.S. government began asking the Indians to leave Nebraska. By several treaties the Pawnee sold their lands to the government. In 1876 the Pawnee were moved by the government to Oklahoma (o • kla • HO • ma). Many died on the trip.

The Ponca Indians were sent to Oklahoma, too, where many died. And the last of the Oto Indians—who had given the state its name—were sent out of Nebraska in 1881.

The Sioux Indians fought for their land. The Sioux chief, Crazy Horse, said: "One does not sell the earth upon which the people walk." In Montana Crazy Horse and his Indians beat George Custer in a famous battle known as "Custer's Last Stand." Crazy Horse and his

Crazy Horse Monument at Fort Robinson

people fought bravely. But there was no way that the Indians could win. U.S. soldiers had forts. They had cannons. Finally, the Sioux were beaten. In 1877 the great Crazy Horse was stabbed to death by a soldier. Crazy Horse had come to surrender at Fort Robinson, in Nebraska. Many people felt that Crazy Horse was murdered, but some said he was trying to escape. After 1879 the Indian wars were over in Nebraska.

The settlers had other problems. In the 1870s grasshoppers swarmed into Nebraska. They ate the crops. There were so many grasshoppers that at times the sky turned dark from them. People had to close their windows (and mouths) so that grasshoppers wouldn't fly in. Some people left Nebraska because of the grasshoppers. Most stayed and waited for the grasshoppers to leave. The worst grasshopper plague (PLAYG) was in 1874. Nebraska has had other grasshopper plagues, one in the 1930s.

One of the worst winters in the history of the United States was in 1888. There was a big blizzard on January 12 in Nebraska. Many people died. Many cattle froze to death. But Nebraskans survived that tough winter.

Nebraskans started to argue among themselves in the 1880s. In eastern Nebraska the people were mostly farmers. But in western Nebraska many people had cattle ranches. Ranchers and cowboys raised the cattle. The cattle were then sold for meat.

As long as the farmers were in the east and the cattlemen in the west, things were fine. Then the farmers started moving westward. They started farming where the cattle grazed. The cattlemen and farmers argued. Sometimes they fought. The cattlemen cut the farmers' fences. They wouldn't let the cattlemen take their cattle to the rivers. The cattlemen called the farmers "nesters." They sometimes burned the houses of the farmers. There were gunfights. There were lynchings.

Cattle
roundup

There were more farmers than cattlemen. The cattlemen were slowly driven out. However, much of western Nebraska wasn't good for farming. After 1904 cattlemen returned. Now their ranches were much smaller.

In 1876 the city of Omaha became a meat-packing center. Many trains went in and out of Omaha. Cattle were shipped to the Union (YOON • yun) Stockyards in Omaha. The meat-packing plants sent meat by train to many places. Thousands of people came from all over to work in Omaha's meat-packing plants. By 1900, 102,555 people lived in Omaha.

You have seen all the tough times Nebraskans had. As
a result, Nebraskans became an independent, straight-
forward people. They don't like waste of any kind. In
1934 Nebraska formed a new kind of state government.
It is called the *unicameral* system. Most states have two
houses where lawmakers meet. One is called the House.
The other is the Senate. Nebraska has only one house.
The unicameral system saves time. It saves money.
Nebraska is the only state with this system. There are
no political parties in the unicameral legislature.

In the 1940s Nebraska farmers began to make more
profits. The United States needed food for soldiers
during World War II.

Harvesting crops

In the 1950s farms in Nebraska became bigger. But
there were fewer farms. And there were fewer farmers.
Nebraska people were moving to Omaha and other cities
in Nebraska. By 1970 three out of every five Nebraskans
lived in a city.

Yet Nebraska is still a farming state. Thanks to the
farmers, many city people earn their living. Some city
people work in factories where vegetables are canned.
Thousands work at turning Nebraska livestock into meat
products. Others work in milk and ice cream plants.

You have learned about some of Nebraska's history. Now it is time to take a trip—in words and pictures— through the Cornhusker State.

If you were in an airplane flying west to east in Nebraska you could see the lay of the land. The land is mostly a flat plain. See that blue river winding like a cowboy's rope across the state? That's the Platte River.

Look down through your airplane window. In western Nebraska you see fields that look like gold. In June western Nebraska has many fields of gold-colored wheat. There are also a lot of cattle ranches in the state.

There is an area in the north central part of Nebraska called the "Sand Hills." It has sand dunes which are held in place by grasses. There are many cattle ranches here.

In eastern Nebraska you'll see many farms. Farmers in the east grow corn, soybeans, oats, and alfalfa. They raise hogs. Nebraska's largest cities are mostly in the eastern half of the state.

Omaha

Your airplane is coming down over a big city in
eastern Nebraska. This is Omaha. Omaha lies on the
banks of the Missouri River. It is Nebraska's biggest
city. Over 375,000 people live in Omaha.

Long ago, the Omaha and other Indians lived here.

In the 1820s fur traders and trappers came to this
area. Omaha became a city in 1854. That year the Omaha
Indians made a treaty giving the land to the United
States. The new settlers named their new city after the
Indians. Farmers came to Omaha. Storekeepers came.
The town was quickly built. It grew, for several reasons.

Gold miners, on their way out west, often stopped in Omaha to buy supplies. More stores were needed, and more storekeepers.

In 1869 the Union Pacific Railroad opened. Farmers sent their crops to Omaha. Then they were sent by train to other places. Omaha became a center for the buying and selling of farm crops.

Many people made a lot of money in Omaha in those days. Omaha was a rough-and-tumble town in the 1880s. Rich people gambled in saloons like the Diamond Gambling House. Sometimes there were gunfights.

Omaha is one of the biggest cattle markets in the world. That means many cattle are bought and sold here. It is one of the world's biggest meat-packing cities. That means a lot of meat is processed here. Some people think

Meat packing

Left: The SAC Museum
Above: Woodmen Tower

of Omaha as still being the rough-and-tumble town it was 100 years ago. It is not. It is a quiet, modern city.

Omaha is called the "Insurance Capital of America." The biggest building in Omaha is Woodmen Tower. It is 30 stories high. It belongs to an insurance company.

The Strategic (strah • TEE • gik) Air Command (SAC) has its headquarters at Offutt Air Force Base, near Omaha. The SAC helps protect our country from attack. There are guided missiles. There are bombers and other airplanes. They are always ready in case our country needs them. About 15,000 people work here.

Visit the Strategic Air Command Aerospace Museum near Omaha. It shows the history of the SAC.

Above: The Brothers Statue at
Boys Town
Right: Students pose at the
entrance sign.

A very famous home for boys was started in 1917 by
Father Edward J. Flanagan, in Omaha. Father Flanagan
believed "there is no such thing as a bad boy." He
borrowed $90 from a friend. He rented a big house in
Omaha. He took in boys who had no homes. He took in
boys who had been in trouble. He gave them a home. He
taught them. Soon, there were so many boys in the house
that Father Flanagan had to find a bigger place. He
finally moved to a farm ten miles from Omaha. He called
the little city that grew up there "Boys Town." You can
visit Boys Town. The students there will show you
around.

Joslyn Art Museum

If you like art, go to the Joslyn Art Museum in Omaha. It has a great Western art collection.

Omaha is also home to the World Series of college baseball, every June. Omaha was always a big baseball city. The "Omaha Wonder," Charles Nichols, won 36 games for a pro team that played there in the 1880s. Bob Gibson was another great baseball player from Omaha.

Every September the Ak-Sar-Ben Rodeo and Livestock Show is held in Omaha. Ak-Sar-Ben is a huge club for Omaha people. Spell Ak-Sar-Ben backwards.

31

Winter
in Lincoln

Lincoln is about 50 miles southwest of Omaha. Lincoln
is the capital of Nebraska. And it is Nebraska's second
biggest city.

The first settlers came to the area in 1856. The town
that grew here was made capital of Nebraska in 1867. It
was named Lincoln, after Abraham Lincoln.

Nebraska lawmakers meet in Lincoln. They meet in
the State Capitol Building. You can see the capitol on the
Nebraska plains, 25 miles away.

Visit the beautiful capitol. It is one of the seven
architectural wonders of the world. It has bright-colored
art works. A sculpture on the building is called "Spirit of
the Pioneers." It shows pioneers going to Nebraska in a

Left: The State Capitol Building
Above: The University of Nebraska at Lincoln

covered wagon. On top of the tower is a statue called the "Sower." It shows a 19-foot-tall bronze farmer planting seeds.

If the state lawmakers are meeting, you can go to watch them. The governor of Nebraska has his office in the capitol, too.

The main home of the University of Nebraska is at Lincoln. Students can learn many things. Some learn about farming. Today, farming is a science. Students learn about the best farming methods. The university is famous for its football team, the Cornhuskers. Over 76,000 people go to see the 'Huskers play on a Saturday. That's about half as many people as live in Lincoln.

33

Above: Elephant Hall
Right: The Lincoln Zoo

Visit the Nebraska State Museum in Lincoln. In
"Elephant Hall" you can see the skeleton of the biggest
mammoth ever found.

At the Children's Zoo, in Lincoln, you can touch many ·
animals that are alive.

In August and September, the Nebraska State Fair is
held in Lincoln. During the State Fair farmers show
their animals. And they show their crops.

There is one little-known fact about Lincoln you might
remember. One of the first black baseball teams, the
Lincoln Giants, played there in the late 1800s. This was
before black players were allowed in the major leagues.

Nebraska has no other cities nearly as big as Omaha or Lincoln.

Grand Island is the third biggest city. It is near the Platte River. Grand Island is an important farming and manufacturing city. There is rich soil near Grand Island. Corn is grown in the area. Food products—such as sugar beets—are packed in Grand Island. Cattle are raised in nearby ranches. Cattle are bought and sold in Grand Island. Grand Island has packing houses where meat is processed. Wire fences and farm equipment are made here. All these products are sent by train to other parts of the United States.

Grand Island is north of the Platte River. Hastings is straight south of Grand Island, and about ten miles south

The Stuhr Museum on Grand Island

Ash Hollow (above left) and Scotts Bluff National Monument (above right) on the Oregon Trail

of the Platte. Hastings is Nebraska's sixth largest city. Corn, wheat, and soybeans are grown near Hastings. They are sent from Hastings to other places by train and truck. Farm equipment is made in Hastings. Baking goods and women's dresses are made here, too.

Once, the Oregon Trail passed near Hastings. You can still see marks made by wagon wheels. Many people died on the trip over the trail. One young woman who died was named Susan Hale. Her husband traveled 250 miles to get a grave marker for her. Then he traveled 250 miles back. According to the story, he pushed the stone in a wheelbarrow all that way! You can still see Susan Hale's grave. It reminds people of the hardships of the pioneers.

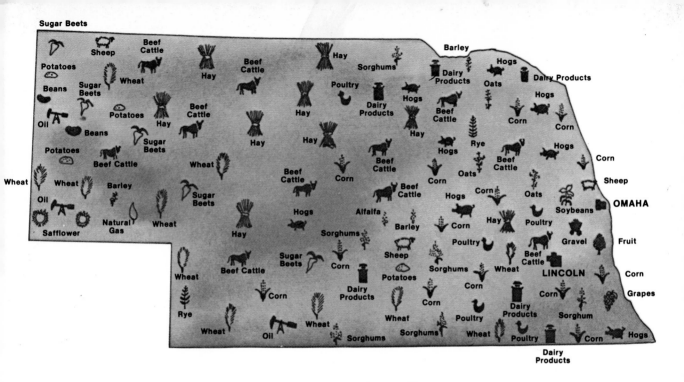

Omaha, Lincoln, Grand Island, North Platte, Freemont, and Hastings are the six biggest cities in Nebraska. All but North Platte are in the eastern half of the state. As you go farther west, the towns are smaller. There is more space between the towns, too. You'll see fields of wheat. You'll see cattle ranches.

A good way to go west through Nebraska is along Interstate 80. It is near the Platte River. Long ago, the Indians traveled this route. They called it the Big Medicine Trail. Later, the Oregon and Mormon trails were built here. The Pony Express went this way. And so did Nebraska's first railroad.

37

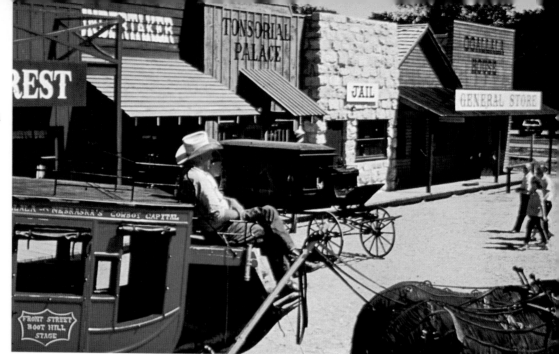

Ogallala

Ogallala (o • ga • LOL • la) is an interesting town to visit in western Nebraska. It used to be a cowboy town. In the 1870s cowboys drove cattle from Texas up to Ogallala and other Nebraska towns. From these towns the cattle were taken by train to bigger cities. Ogallala was a real wild-west town in those days. The cowboys were ready for action after the long cattle drives. Ogallala had saloons. Cowboys gambled for gold. They had fist fights. There were gunfights, too. Some were right out on the street, like in a Western movie.

There are many rodeos in western Nebraska towns. North Platte Nebraskaland Days is held every June.

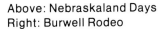
Above: Nebraskaland Days
Right: Burwell Rodeo

"Buffalo Bill" Cody had a ranch near North Platte. He was an Indian fighter. He killed a lot of buffalo for food for railroad workers. That was how he earned his nickname. Later in life he formed a "Wild West Show."

Being a cowboy is very hard work. Cowboys have to round up cattle. They have to brand them. They have to feed cattle and get them ready for market. They have to fix fences. Cattle ranches are a big business. Cowboys are an important part of that business. There are about nine million head of cattle in Nebraska. That makes six for each person.

39

Scotts Bluff
on the
Oregon Trail

Western Nebraska has a lot of rugged land. There are hills. There are patches of evergreen trees. And there are weird-looking rocks, called *buttes* (BYOOTS). You can see Chimney Rock from many miles away. The Indians thought it looked more like a tepee. It was a landmark on the Oregon Trail. Another famous landmark is Scotts Bluff. Pioneers climbed it to see the nearby countryside. It was named for a fur trader named Hiram Scott. At Toadstool Park, in northwest Nebraska, there are some rocks that look like giant mushrooms.

Many of Nebraska's wild animals live in the western part of the state. Deer, geese, antelope, coyotes, and prairie dogs live there. There are few buffalo left.

A number of famous people have lived in Nebraska. Gerald R. Ford grew up in Michigan (MISH • a • gen). But he was born in Omaha. As a young man, he was a star football player. Later, he became 38th president of the United States.

Julius Sterling Morton came to live in Nebraska City when he was twenty-three years old. He became a Nebraska lawmaker. Morton felt trees were needed on the Great Plains. He planted trees on his own property. Then Morton said that everyone in Nebraska should plant trees on a certain day. Morton called this tree-planting day *Arbor Day*. On the first Arbor Day, in 1872, about a million trees were planted in Nebraska. Later, Arbor Day became a day for tree-planting in many states.

A number of actors came from Nebraska, too. Henry Fonda was born in Grand Island. The great dancer-actor-singer Fred Astaire was born in Omaha. The actor Marlon Brando was born in Omaha, too.

Willa Cather's home

The grave of Mari Sandoz

Some famous authors have lived in Nebraska. Willa Cather came to live in Red Cloud when she was nine. She wrote stories about pioneers. She wrote *O Pioneers* and *One of Ours*. Mari Sandoz grew up in the Sand Hills area of Nebraska. She wrote Western books. Two of her books are *Cheyenne Autumn* and *Crazy Horse*.

The land where mammoths roamed . . . Indians hunted for buffalo . . . and Spanish explorers looked for gold.

A place where hardy pioneers built their houses right out of the ground.

Birthplace of a United States president.

Now a modern state of farming . . . cattle raising . . . and business.

This is the Cornhusker State — Nebraska.

Facts About NEBRASKA

Area—77,237 square miles (15th biggest state)

Greatest Distance North to South—205 miles

Greatest Distance East to West—415 miles

Border States—South Dakota on the north; Missouri and Iowa on the east across the Missouri River; Colorado and Kansas on the south; Wyoming and Colorado on the west

Highest Point—5,426 feet above sea level (in Kimball County)

Lowest Point—840 feet above sea level (in Richardson County)

Hottest Recorded Temperature—118° (recorded in three different places)

Coldest Recorded Temperature—Minus 47° (at Camp Clarke, on February 12, 1899)

Statehood—Our 37th state, on March 1, 1867

Origin of Name Nebraska—From the Oto Indian word *Nebrathka,* which means *flat water* and refers to the Platte River

Capital—Lincoln (1867)

Counties—93

U.S. Senators—2

U.S. Representatives—3

Electoral Votes—5

State Legislature—There are 49 members of the unicameral legislature

State Song—"Beautiful Nebraska" by Jim Fras and Guy Miller

State Motto—*Equality Before the Law*

Nicknames—Cornhusker State, Beef State, Tree Planters' State

State Seal—Adopted in 1867

State Flag—Adopted in 1925

State Flower—Goldenrod

State Bird—Western meadowlark

State Tree—Cottonwood

State Rock—Prairie agate

State Gem Stone—Blue agate

State Fossil—Mammoth

State Insect—Honey bee

Some Colleges and Universities—Doane College, Creighton University, Hastings College, University of Nebraska, Nebraska Wesleyan University, Union College

Principal River—Platte

Some Other Rivers—Missouri, North Platte, South Platte, Loup, Elkhorn, Big Blue, Little Blue, Republican, Niobrara

State Parks—5

Animals—Whitetail deer, mule deer, antelope, prairie dogs, coyotes, badgers, raccoons, rabbits, skunks, grouse, ducks, geese, pheasants, quail, prairie chickens

Fishing—Catfish, bass, carp, perch, trout, pike

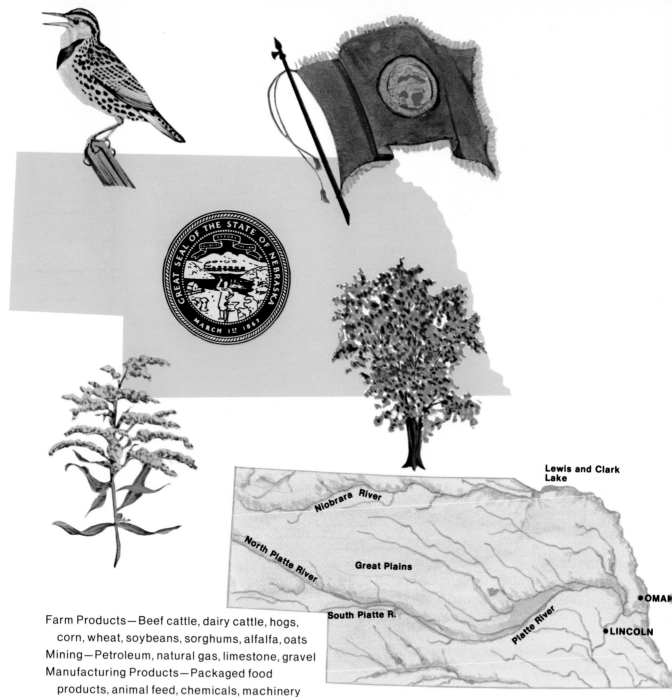

Farm Products—Beef cattle, dairy cattle, hogs,
   corn, wheat, soybeans, sorghums, alfalfa, oats
Mining—Petroleum, natural gas, limestone, gravel
Manufacturing Products—Packaged food
   products, animal feed, chemicals, machinery
Population—1980 census: 1,569,825 (1993 estimate: 1,610,000)

Major Cities	1980 Census	1990 Estimate
Omaha	313,926	294,242
Lincoln	171,932	183,871
Grand Island	33,180	32,770
North Platte	24,509	23,365
Freemont	23,979	23,692
Hastings	23,045	22,791

44

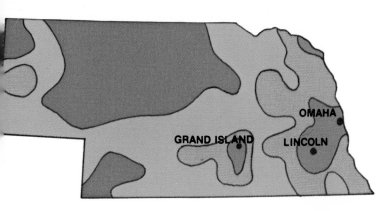

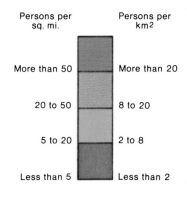

Persons per sq. mi.	Persons per km2
More than 50	More than 20
20 to 50	8 to 20
5 to 20	2 to 8
Less than 5	Less than 2

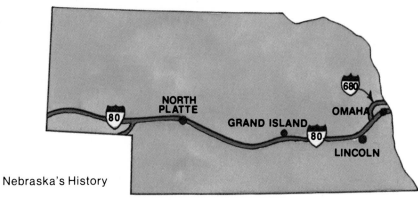

Nebraska's History

The earliest people in Nebraska—including the Folsom Culture—lived there at least 12,000 years ago. People may have been in Nebraska over 25,000 years ago.

1541—Coronado, looking for a city of gold, crosses plains in Nebraska region. Because of Coronado and other Spanish explorers, Spain claims Nebraska

1682—The Frenchman La Salle claims a huge area, including Nebraska, for France

1714—French explorer de Bourgmont explores mouth of Platte River

1720—Pawnee Indians defeat Spanish, killing Spanish leader Pedro de Villasur

1739—The Mallet brothers explore the Platte River

1763—Spain controls Nebraska

1801—France again controls Nebraska by official treaty

1803—The United States buys land, including Nebraska, from France

1804—Meriwether Lewis and William Clark explore eastern Nebraska; they meet with Missouri and Oto Indians

1806—Nebraska is explored by American Zebulon M. Pike

1812—Manuel Lisa establishes Fort Lisa, 10 miles from Omaha

1819—Fort Atkinson is founded by U.S. Army

1823—Bellevue, first permanent settlement in Nebraska, is begun

1830—Sublette and companions make first wagon road across Nebraska

1842 — John Frémont and Kit Carson cross Nebraska on Oregon Trail

1846-59 — Mormons, crossing Nebraska, form Mormon Trail on north side of Platte River

1854 — Nebraska Territory is created; Omaha City becomes capital

1858 — J. Sterling Morton, founder of Arbor Day, is acting governor of Nebraska Territory

1860 — Pony Express goes through Nebraska

1863 — On January 1, Daniel Freeman starts first free homestead under Homestead Act, near Beatrice

1866 — Cattle ranching business begun in western Nebraska

1867 — On March 1 Nebraska becomes the 37th state; Lincoln is the capital; David Butler is first governor

1869 — Union Pacific Railroad, built through Nebraska in 1867, is opened

1870 — Population is 122,993

1871 — University of Nebraska is opened

1872 — J. Sterling Morton begins Arbor Day, in Nebraska

1874 — Sioux Indians surrender; their great chief, Crazy Horse, is killed

1875-77 — Pawnee Indians forced in leave Nebraska

1880 — Population of Nebraska is 452,402

1880's — "Sodbusters" and cattlemen arguing in western Nebraska

1881 — Oto Indians forced to leave Nebraska

1888 — Terrible winter; blizzards kill many people and livestock in Nebraska

1890 — Year of drought (little rain) causes crops to die; population of Nebraska is 1,062,656

1898 — Trans-Mississippi Exposition held in Omaha

1900 — Population of Nebraska is 1,066,300

1904 — By Kinkaid Act homesteaders can get 640 acres of free land in western Nebraska

1913 — Gerald Ford is born on July 14 in Omaha

1917 — Boys Town started by Father Flanagan in Omaha

1917 — U.S. enters World War I; 47,801 Nebraskans fight

1930 — 1,377,963 people live in Nebraska

1934 — Nebraskans vote to have unicameral legislature

1939 — Oil is discovered in Nebraska, Richardson County

1941 — U.S. enters World War II; 120,000 Nebraskans serve

1944 — Missouri River Basin Project begun to build dams and electricity plants

1948 — Strategic Air Command builds headquarters near Omaha

1967 — Happy 100th birthday, Cornhusker State!

1974 — Gerald Ford, born in Omaha, becomes the 38th president of the United States

1975 — Omaha tornado costs $223 million

1985 — Dry, hot weather causes record infestations of grasshoppers

1987 — Kay Orr becomes the state's first woman governor

1989 — President Bush test drives a clean fuel car powered with a mixture of gasoline and ethanol at a Nebraska plant

1991 — Ben Nelson is elected governor

INDEX

About the Author:

Dennis Fradin attended Northwestern University on a creative writing scholarship and was graduated in 1967. While still at Northwestern, he published his first stories in *Ingenue* magazine and also won a prize in *Seventeen's* short story competition. A prolific writer, Dennis Fradin has been regularly publishing stories in such diverse places as *The Saturday Evening Post, Scholastic, National Humane Review, Midwest,* and *The Teaching Paper.* He has also scripted several educational films. Since 1970 he has taught second grade reading in a Chicago school—a rewarding job, which, the author says, "provides a captive audience on whom I test my children's stories." Married and the father of two children, Dennis Fradin spends his free time with his family or playing a myriad of sports and games with his childhood chums.

About the Artists:

Len Meents studied painting and drawing at Southern Illinois University and after graduation in 1969 he moved to Chicago. Mr. Meents works full time as a painter and illustrator. He and his wife and child currently make their home in LaGrange, Illinois.

Richard Wahl, graduate of the Art Center College of Design in Los Angeles, has illustrated a number of magazine articles and booklets. He is a skilled artist and photographer who advocates realistic interpretations of his subjects. He lives with his wife and two sons in Libertyville, Illinois.